My First Chinese Picture Books for Short Sentences Book 3

我的第一套中文短句绘本 3

Xiaolin Huang

To Cooper and Danna for being the pilot readers

First Published in Australia in 2017
This edition published in 2017
by Xiaolin Huang
ABN 60 520 297 573

Copyright Xiaolin Huang 2017
127 Cambridge Cres
Wyndham Vale
VIC 3024, Australia

http://fb.me/mfcpb

National Library of Australia Cataloguing-in-Publication entry

Creator: Huang, Xiaolin, author.

Title: My first Chinese picture books for short sentences. Book 3 : 我的第一套中文短句绘本 第三册 / Xiaolin Huang.

ISBN: 9780648102533 (paperback)

Target Audience: For preschool age

Subjects: Chinese characters--Juvenile literature
Chinese language--Writing--Juvenile literature
Chinese language--Juvenile literature
Picture books for children

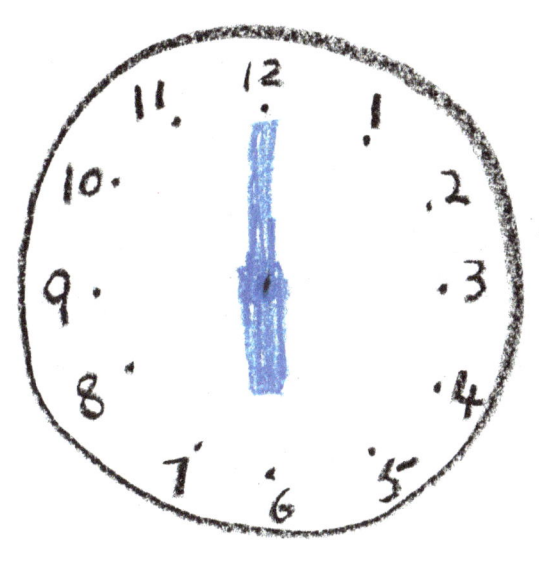

现在是六点钟

现在是七点半

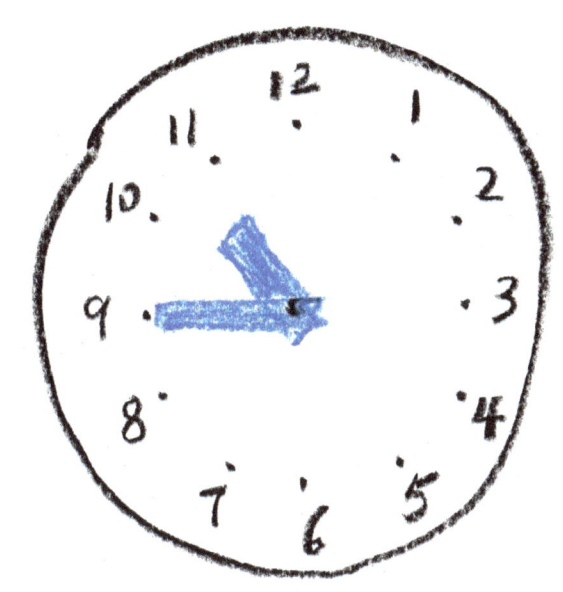

现在是上午
十点四十五

我在下午五点半
吃晚饭

我在晚上八点洗澡

哥哥早上九点钟上课

今天是星期三

昨天是星期二

明天是星期四

星期五我去学校

星期六我去游乐场

星期天我去教堂

我喜欢春天

我喜欢夏天

我喜欢秋天

我喜欢冬天

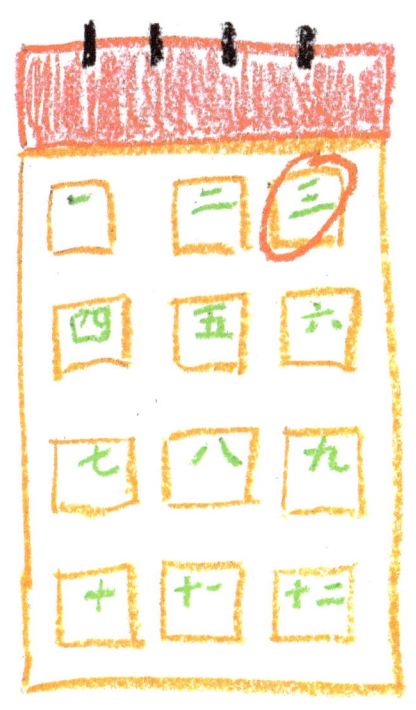

我喜欢三月

我喜欢二月,
因为二月过中国新年

我喜欢十二月，
因为十二月有圣诞节

完

The End

本书常见字 你能认识几个

Frequently Used Characters
Try to recognise and read

年	在	六
七	上	去
中	八	早
月	是	点
四	九	五

www.ingramcontent.com/pod-product-compliance
Lightning Source LLC
Chambersburg PA
CBHW061822290426
44110CB00027B/2953